TRADE & RELIGION

Barbarian Invasions, Empires around the
World & Medieval Europe, AD 456–1450

Cover: The first modern European
bank was established in Venice in 1171 in
order to lend money to the government.

Kingfisher Books, Grisewood & Dempsey Ltd,
Elsley House, 24–30 Great Titchfield Street,
London W1P 7AD

First published in paperback in 1991 by Kingfisher Books
Originally published in hardback in 1990 by Kingfisher Books
10 9 8 7 6 5 4 3 2 1

BRITISH LIBRARY CATALOGUING IN PUBLICATION DATA

Adams, Simon
   Trade and religion.
   1. Religion. History   2. Trade. History
I. Title   II. Kramer, Ann   III. Series
200.9

ISBN 0-86272-758-8

Editors: Nicola Barber and Annabel Warburg
Series editor: Ann Kramer
Series designer: Robert Wheeler
Maps: Eugene Fleury and Malcolm Porter
Illustrations: Kevin Maddison and Stephen Conlin
Picture research: Elaine Willis
Phototypeset by Rowland Phototypesetting Ltd, Bury St Edmunds, Suffolk
Printed and bound in Spain

HISTORICAL ATLAS

TRADE & RELIGION

Barbarian Invasions, Empires around the World & Medieval Europe, AD 456–1450

SIMON ADAMS & ANN KRAMER

Kingfisher Books

Contents

Introduction

This book tells the story of the world from
the end of the Roman Empire to the start of
the Reformation. It covers the break-up of
the Roman and Chinese Empires after the
nomadic invasions, the attempts by the
Byzantine Empire and Charlemagne to
rebuild the Roman Empire, the spread of
Christianity and Buddhism and the rise of
Islam, the Viking and Mongol invasions, the
empires of America, Africa and Asia, and
the growth of European cities.

But history is not just about dates and
events. It is about people and how they
lived in the past. Using colourful
illustrations, *Trade and Religion* takes a
close look at the daily lives of people
during this period and the discoveries and
inventions they made. Feature pages
examine Arab learning and science, how
people travelled, why castles were built, the
impact of the Black Death, and the
technological developments of the period.

Trade and Religion is divided up into
five chapters. The first shows the world as
it was in 450. The following chapters tell
the history of different periods of time and
different regions of the world. Difficult
words in the text are highlighted in **bold**
and are explained in the Glossary, while a
Timeline at the end of the book provides a
list of key dates.

Some dates are not known exactly, so are
marked *c.* for *circa*, meaning 'about'.

The World in 450 and After

The world in 450

About 2000 years ago, most people in the world lived within four great **empires**. The Roman Empire was the most powerful, and controlled Europe and north Africa. To the east, the Han **Dynasty** (family) governed much of what is now modern China. Between them lay the rich Sassanian Empire in the Middle East, and the great Gupta Empire of India.

These powerful empires were secure and peaceful, with strong governments and wealthy **economies**. **Trade** linked them all together. Land travel was slow, however, and many goods were transported on boats, which crossed both the Indian Ocean and the Mediterranean Sea. These trading contacts brought the peoples of the four empires together and helped the spread of religious and other ideas.

These links did not stretch across either the Pacific or Atlantic Oceans. As a result, the peoples of Australia and America developed **cultures** of their own. Much of Africa, too, developed independently of the rest of the world.

By 450 the great empires of the world were under threat from various warlike **tribes** of **nomads** in northern Europe and parts of Asia. Within a few years these tribes were to disrupt the settled empires.

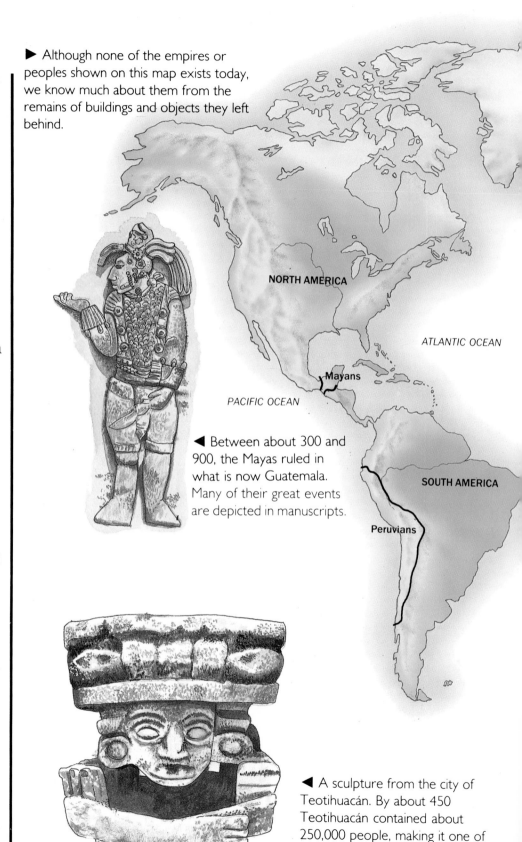

► Although none of the empires or peoples shown on this map exists today, we know much about them from the remains of buildings and objects they left behind.

◄ Between about 300 and 900, the Mayas ruled in what is now Guatemala. Many of their great events are depicted in manuscripts.

◄ A sculpture from the city of Teotihuacán. By about 450 Teotihuacán contained about 250,000 people, making it one of the biggest cities in the world at that time.

8

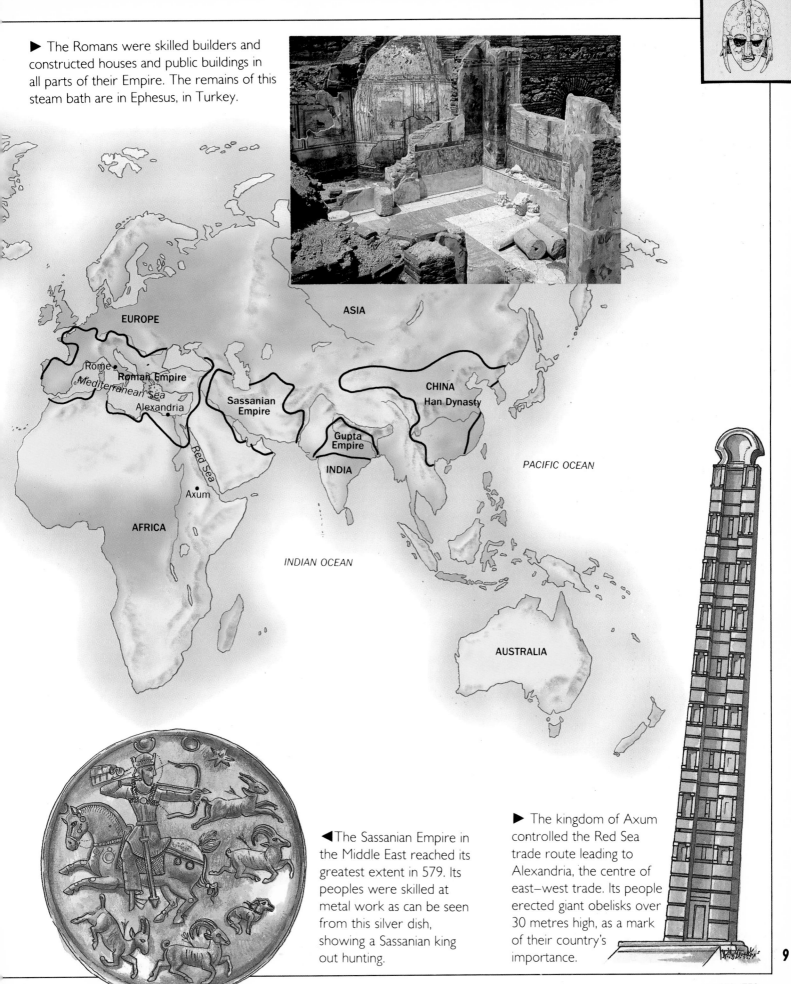

▶ The Romans were skilled builders and constructed houses and public buildings in all parts of their Empire. The remains of this steam bath are in Ephesus, in Turkey.

EUROPE

ASIA

Rome
Roman Empire
Mediterranean Sea
Alexandria

Sassanian
Empire

CHINA
Han Dynasty

Gupta
Empire

INDIA

Red Sea

Axum

AFRICA

PACIFIC OCEAN

INDIAN OCEAN

AUSTRALIA

◀The Sassanian Empire in the Middle East reached its greatest extent in 579. Its peoples were skilled at metal work as can be seen from this silver dish, showing a Sassanian king out hunting.

▶ The kingdom of Axum controlled the Red Sea trade route leading to Alexandria, the centre of east–west trade. Its people erected giant obelisks over 30 metres high, as a mark of their country's importance.

9

The collapse of empires

Ever since 200BC, the four empires in Europe and Asia had come under threat from heavily armed nomadic tribes. The Romans called them **Barbarians**, for they were not educated and were not Christians. Nor did they live in settled towns but in tents on the vast **steppes** of central Asia. They travelled thousands of miles in search of grazing land, and when the **pasture** land was exhausted, or if they were attacked by rival tribes, they moved in search of new land, threatening the settled empires to the south and west.

At first, both the Romans and Chinese kept the nomads out, building strong defences such as Hadrian's Wall in Britain and the Great Wall in China. These defences were expensive and the high **taxes** imposed to pay for them caused rebellions which weakened both the Chinese and Roman Empires.

China was the first empire to fall. In 220, the Hsiungnu peoples of central Asia attacked China and ended Han rule in the country. The Huns, part of the Hsiungnu tribe, killed the Persian Emperor in 484, and by 535 had destroyed the Gupta Empire in India.

But it was the Roman Empire that suffered the most. Tribes had attacked the Roman Empire as early as 167, but after 370 the attacks were more serious and Rome was overrun. In 476, the last Roman Emperor was overthrown and the Empire was replaced by small tribal kingdoms.

▲ Because little written evidence exists about the fall of the Roman Empire, we have to learn about it from craftworks, buildings and carvings. This carving is on the side of a tomb dating from around 200, and shows Roman soldiers fighting German invaders.

▶ The peoples who invaded the Roman Empire were skilled craft workers. This elaborate helmet of iron, bronze and silver was made by the Saxon invaders of Britain in about 625.

▼ Many of the tribes that invaded the Roman Empire adopted its official religion of Christianity. This gold helmet plaque shows an Ostrogoth ruler surrounded by angels.

450–750

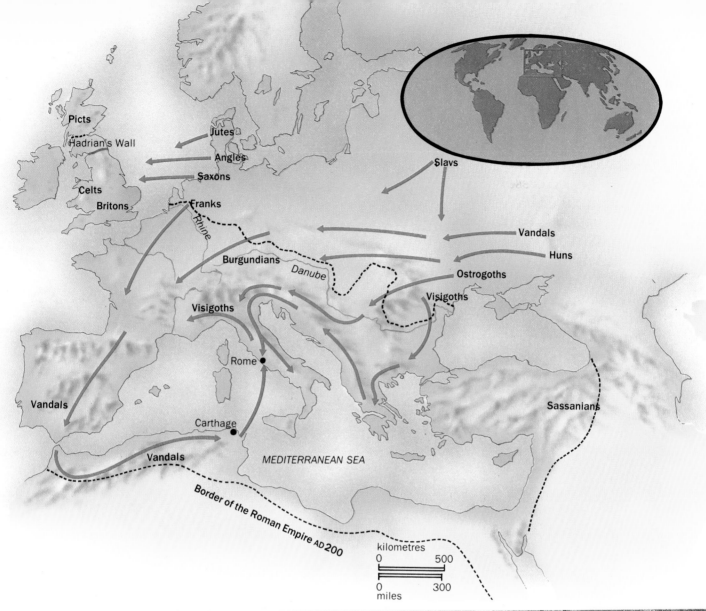

▲ From about 167 a number of warring tribes attacked the long land frontier of the Roman Empire in central Europe. At first they were kept out of the Empire. But when the Huns arrived in eastern Europe from central Asia around 370, many tribes started pouring over the frontier. The Visigoths sacked Rome in 410 and moved on to settle in southern Spain, while the Vandals moved into Spain by 409 and north Africa in 429. In the north, the Franks settled in what is now France, while the Angles, Saxons and Jutes invaded Britain.

▶ The Vandals invaded north Africa and set up their capital at Carthage. They took over the existing city and lived in the Roman houses, adopting Roman clothes and ways of life. This **mosaic**, made in about 500, shows a Vandal warrior leaving his villa as if he were a Roman citizen, not a conqueror.

11

The Byzantine Empire

In 284, Diocletian became Roman Emperor. He decided that the huge Empire could only be ruled effectively by splitting it into two parts, east and west. In 330 his successor, Constantine, rebuilt the old Greek port of Byzantium, at the entrance to the Black Sea, and renamed it Constantinople. This city became the capital of the eastern half of the Empire. When the western half collapsed during the next century, Constantinople became the capital of the new Byzantine Empire.

At first, this Empire only controlled a small area around the eastern Mediterranean, but during the reign of Justinian (527–65), it started to recover much of the territory of the old Roman Empire. North Africa, Italy and southern Spain were all reconquered.

The Byzantine Empire was wealthy, producing gold, silk, grain, olives and wine, and these were traded for spices, precious stones, furs and ivory with countries as far afield as China and India. The Empire was a centre of learning, combining the knowledge of the Ancient Greeks with the newer teachings of the Christian Church.

However, by 750, the last invaders from the east – Bulgars, Slavs and Lombards – reduced the Empire to a small area of what is now Greece and Turkey, and it never regained its strength. Yet it lasted until 1453, when the city of Constantinople was finally captured by the Turks.

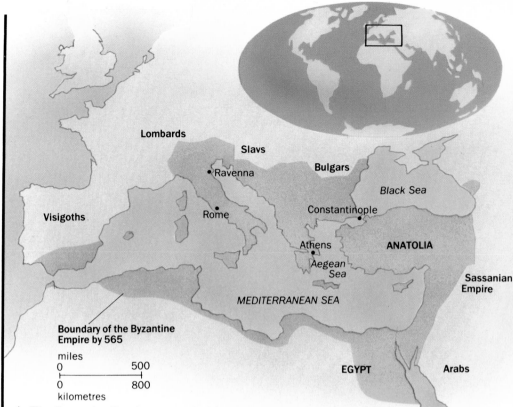

▲ The Byzantine Empire was ruled from its capital city of Constantinople, known today as Istanbul. At first the Empire lay around the Aegean Sea. It reached its greatest extent under Justinian, when it spread across the Mediterranean to Spain. However, it was always under threat from its warlike neighbours.

▼ This old map of Constantinople shows fortifications and many fine buildings. The city was an important trading centre and commanded both the sea route between the Mediterranean and the Black Sea, and the land route between Europe and Asia and on to China.

▼ Many churches and public buildings in the Byzantine Empire were decorated with elaborate mosaics. These were made of thousands of coloured glass cubes set in plaster. Some of the cubes were covered with gold or silver dust to make them glisten in the light.

▼ The Byzantine Empire was often under attack both from sea and from land. The secret weapon of the Byzantine navy was 'Greek Fire', a chemical mixture which burst into flames when it touched water.

▲ Under Justinian and Empress Theodora, the Byzantine Empire was a centre for the arts and learning. This mosaic of Justinian is in the church of San Vitale in Ravenna, for a time the capital of the Byzantine Empire in Italy.

The decimal system
Sometime after 400 the Guptas of India developed a new method of counting, which was based on multiples of 10. They used the symbol 0 to represent zero and the symbol . to separate whole numbers from fractions. From this came the decimal system that we use today. The Guptas also designed a simple way of writing numbers down. We call these numbers 'Arabic' numerals, because, like the decimal system, they came to us from the Arabs whose traders learned them in India and brought them to Europe sometime after 1300.

The Religious World

All of the major religions have begun in Asia. Three of them – Judaism, Christianity and **Islam** – started in the Middle East and their followers regard Jerusalem as a holy city. These religions have spread across the world as **missionaries**, traders and other people travelled along the trade routes.

Early Christianity

Christianity began in the Roman province of Judaea, in what is now Israel. Originally it was part of the Jewish religion. But in about AD30, when its founder, Jesus Christ, was put to death by the Romans, his followers became known as Christians and founded a new religion based on the teachings of Christ.

The early Christians travelled throughout the Roman Empire preaching the message of Christ. At first the Romans persecuted them. But in 312 the Roman Emperor Constantine legalized Christianity and it became the official religion of the Roman Empire in 392. Christianity grew in strength because it offered hope to its followers in the troubled times. Many of the invading tribes also adopted Christianity, but it spread slowly, and in some places, such as the British Isles, the early Christians had to struggle to keep the religion alive.

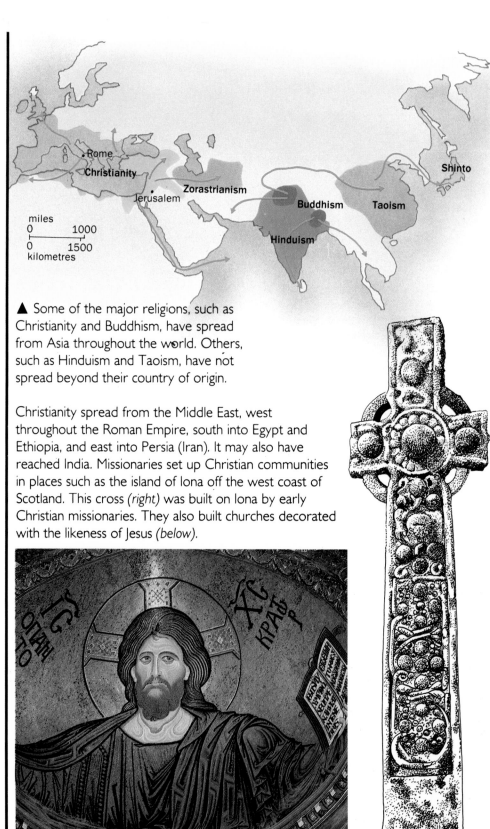

▲ Some of the major religions, such as Christianity and Buddhism, have spread from Asia throughout the world. Others, such as Hinduism and Taoism, have not spread beyond their country of origin.

Christianity spread from the Middle East, west throughout the Roman Empire, south into Egypt and Ethiopia, and east into Persia (Iran). It may also have reached India. Missionaries set up Christian communities in places such as the island of Iona off the west coast of Scotland. This cross (right) was built on Iona by early Christian missionaries. They also built churches decorated with the likeness of Jesus (below).

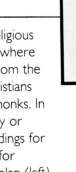

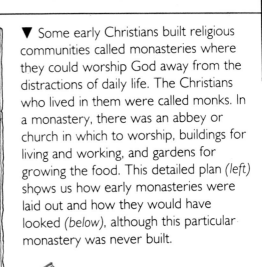

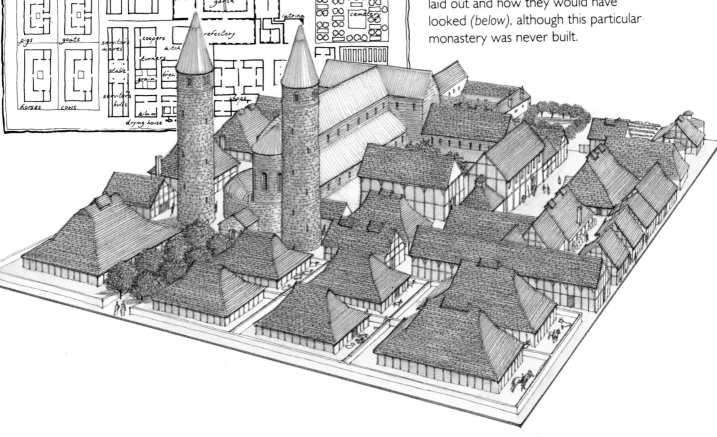

▼ Some early Christians built religious communities called monasteries where they could worship God away from the distractions of daily life. The Christians who lived in them were called monks. In a monastery, there was an abbey or church in which to worship, buildings for living and working, and gardens for growing the food. This detailed plan *(left)* shows us how early monasteries were laid out and how they would have looked *(below)*, although this particular monastery was never built.

► Monasteries were important centres of learning because monks were almost the only people who could read and write. Monks drew up official documents, kept records and wrote letters. They also copied books *(right)*, which was the only way a book could be reproduced, for printing presses were unknown in Europe until 1453. Copying was done by hand and could take many years. Some monks were skilled illustrators, as can be seen from this detail *(far right)* in the beautiful Book of Kells, a religious manuscript which was produced on the Scottish island of Iona in about 800.

The rise of Islam

In the 600s, a new religion began in Arabia. It was called Islam, which means 'Submission to the will of Allah (God)'. Within 100 years, more than half the total population of Europe and Asia was Muslim (the name given to followers of Islam).

Islam was founded by a prophet called Muhammad. He came from the Arabian city of Mecca and in about 610 began to write the Koran, the holy book of Islam. The new religion threatened the old gods worshipped in Mecca, so in 622 Muhammad and his followers were forced to flee to the nearby town of Medina.

From Medina, Muhammad and his followers organized the first Muslim **state** and built the first mosque. Although Arabia was a wealthy region, most of the population was very poor. Many of these poor people were attracted to Islam because its teachings offered them a fairer society.

In 630 Muhammad attacked and captured Mecca. Under his rule, as **Caliph**, Mecca became the capital of an Islamic empire that controlled most of the Arabian peninsula. After Muhammad's death in 632, Muslim armies spread the Islamic religion eastwards to India and westwards across north Africa and into Spain. The Byzantine Empire was seriously weakened and lost all its lands in Africa. But the Muslims were defeated by the Franks in France at the battle of Poitiers in 732 and their empire extended no farther.

▲ The Kaaba in Mecca houses a sacred black stone and is the centre of the Islamic world. At certain times during the day, every Muslim in the world faces towards it to pray. **Pilgrims** to Mecca walk around it seven times in homage.

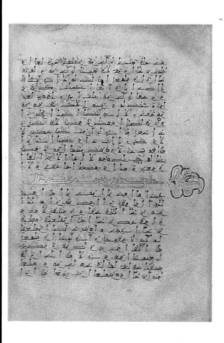

◄ The Koran is the holy book of Islam. Muslims believe that it is the word of God as told to his prophet Muhammad. The Koran contains religious beliefs as well as social and political instructions.

▼ Islam began in Arabia but quickly spread throughout the Middle East and north Africa by 750 (shaded area on map below). Although united by one faith, the Islamic world soon broke up into separate countries.

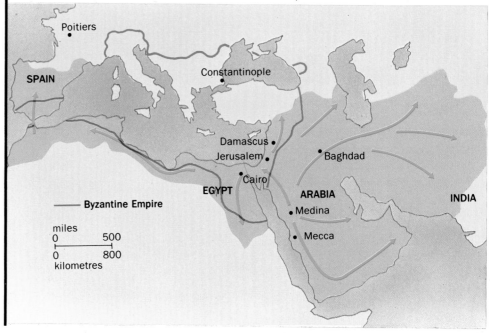

Arab Science and Learning

In 762, Al-Mansur, the leader of the Islamic world, built a new capital city at Baghdad in what is now Iraq. He made it a centre of learning and culture. There was an observatory to study the stars and a 'House of Learning' in which scholars studied mathematics and translated the writings of the Ancient Greeks into Arabic. Christian and Jewish scholars were welcomed because Islam was tolerant of other religions. Cairo, in Egypt, was also a centre of learning, and in 971, the world's first university was opened there. The arts flourished throughout the Islamic world, particularly calligraphy or writing. This was because it was forbidden to draw or paint human figures in religious pictures.

▲ Arab astronomers, like the Ancient Greeks, showed the constellations of the stars as human figures. The constellation shown here is Cepheus.

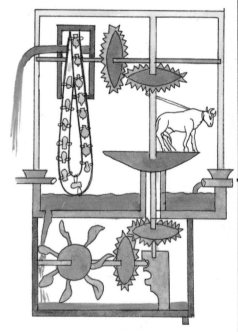

▲ Water was scarce in the hot, dry climate of the Islamic world. Arab engineers were skilled in methods of raising water from the ground and piping it into their homes.

▲ In 1154, Arab map-makers drew this map of the world. It shows that they were familiar with the basic outlines of Asia, north Africa and Europe. But like the Europeans at this time, they did not know that Australia or America existed.

▲ Arab medicine was very advanced. Islamic pharmacists or chemists were skilled in making up suitable drugs for treating illnesses.

The Buddhist world

Buddhism, one of the world's greatest religions, began as an offshoot of Hinduism, an Indian religion that dates back to 1500BC and is still widely practised today. The Hindus divided people up into social classes called **castes**. They believed that a person was born into one particular caste and could not leave it during his or her lifetime. But many people disliked this strict system because it meant that nothing could be changed and that suffering and poverty were allowed to continue.

In about 525BC, an Indian prince called Gautama Siddhartha, who had left his rich family to travel and study, began to preach another message. He said that it was possible to overcome suffering and reach a state of total peace, which he called 'Nirvana'.

By the time of his death in 483BC, Gautama had become known as the Buddha or 'the Enlightened One' and his teachings spread throughout India. In about 257BC, the Indian ruler Asoka became a Buddhist, and Buddhism became a major force throughout southern Asia. Missionaries spread the religion north to Afghanistan, Tibet, China and Japan, where it became the official religion in 594. They also spread Buddhism south to Burma and the rest of Indochina. Buddhism gained strength from the upheavals caused by the nomadic invasions. In 624 Buddhism became the official religion of China.

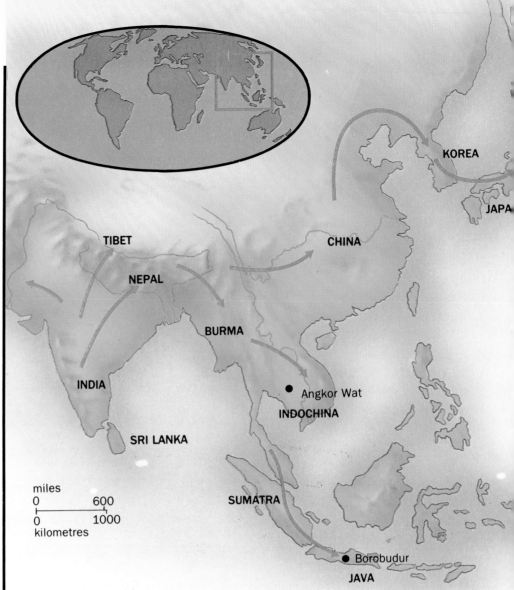

▲ Missionaries spread the Buddhist religion from India north to Afghanistan, Tibet, China, and Japan and south to Burma and Indochina, often following trade routes.

▼ The Buddhist temple of Borobudur in Java was built about 800. It has ten levels. Each level represents the different stages of a person's life from ignorance to Nirvana, the ultimate Buddhist aim.

450–750

► When the Chinese Princess Yung T'ai was only 17, she was forced to commit suicide for criticizing her grandmother, the Chinese Empress Wu (690–713). Yung T'ai's tomb is decorated with portraits of court ladies accompanied by servants waiting on the princess.

▼ During the time of the Sui Dynasty in China (581–618), more than 100,000 statues of Buddha were built, some out of solid rock, and nearly 4000 temples were constructed.

Footbinding
In Chinese culture, small feet were considered a sign of beauty. The daughters of the wealthy classes had their feet bound tightly with silk when they were very young. As they grew up, their feet stayed so small that the women could not walk without considerable pain. Footbinding continued in China almost to the present day.

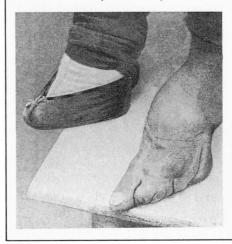

19

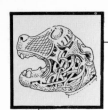

Empires and Invasions

Charlemagne and the Holy Roman Empire

On Christmas Day in 800, the Pope crowned a new Roman Emperor, Charles the Great, or Charlemagne as he is better known.

Charlemagne was a Frank, one of the peoples who had invaded the Roman Empire and settled in what is now central France. The leader of the Franks, Clovis, was a Christian and had founded the Merovingian Dynasty of kings. But following Frankish tradition, the kingdom had been divided between the various royal sons. This weakened it so much that power fell into the hands of leading officials. In 751, one of the officials, Pepin, deposed the Merovingians and formed the Carolingian Dynasty. In 768, Pepin's two sons, Carloman and Charlemagne inherited the kingdom, and in 771, when his brother died, Charlemagne took full control.

Charlemagne soon conquered the rest of France and extended his kingdom into what is now Germany, Italy and The Netherlands. He forcibly converted to Christianity the Saxons and Avars who lived in central Europe. By the time of his death in 814, the Franks were the most powerful force in western Europe.

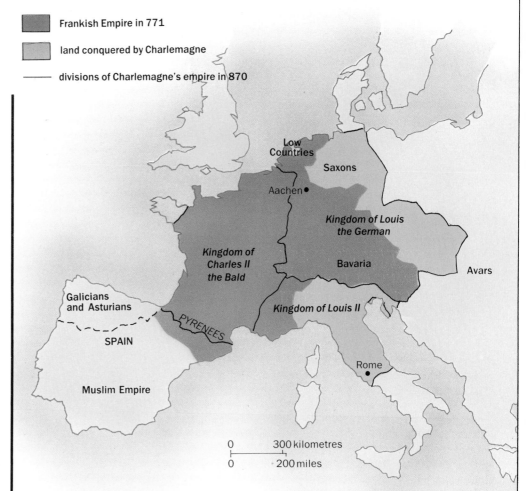

Frankish Empire in 771

land conquered by Charlemagne

— divisions of Charlemagne's empire in 870

The Holy Roman Empire
When Charlemagne was crowned in 800, he founded an empire that later became known as the Holy Roman Empire. This Empire lasted 1000 years until 1806 when it was abolished by the French Emperor, Napoleon Bonaparte. It was revived briefly between 1871 and 1918 when Germany was united as one country for the first time. Between 1933 and 1945, the German dictator, Adolf Hitler, attempted to build a Third Reich (Empire) to last a further 1000 years, but he was defeated.

▲ Charlemagne's empire stretched from northern Spain across Europe to Germany and Italy. When it was divided between his three grandsons in 843, and again in 870, the boundaries of present-day France, Italy and Germany became recognizable for the first time.

▼ The scholars who came to Charlemagne's court at Aachen in Germany developed a new style of handwriting in which to write their books. This was Carolingian **minuscule**, used by the first printers 600 years later when they designed a type in which to print the first books.

BEATISSIMO PAPAE DAMASO
HIERONIMUS

Trade and Transport

Before cars, trains and aeroplanes were invented, most people never left the town or village in which they were born. People worked within walking distance of their houses and no one took holidays away from home. The only people who travelled were soldiers, traders, government officials and pilgrims going to visit religious sites. They walked or rode on horseback along rough roads and their journeys were slow and often dangerous. On land, robbers attacked foot travellers, while pirate raids were common at sea. But despite these problems, many travellers covered great distances and the main roads were often very busy.

◀ Travelling could be hazardous, Here a traveller surrenders his money to a highwayman.

▲ Trade was carried across the Indian Ocean by ships called *dhows*. These simple but safe ships had lots of room for both passengers and cargo.

◀ Merchants, craftworkers and buyers gathered at the fairs which were held in large towns all over Europe. This fair at Lendit in France started off as a religious festival.

▲ The **Silk Road** was the main land route between China and Europe. It was 4000 kilometres long and the best way to travel along it was by camel.

Viking invasions

Peace in western Europe did not last long. After 900, Muslim Arabs from north Africa conquered Italy and crossed the Pyrenees to threaten France. The Magyars, another group of Asian nomads, raided Germany and Italy.

But the most powerful threat came from the Viking peoples of Scandinavia – Sweden, Norway and Denmark. They left their homes in search of wealth and better farmland. They were skilled seafarers, and sailed vast distances in their open longboats.

In 793 the Vikings raided Britain and soon occupied the northern half of the country. They established **colonies** in Ireland, and by 911 had settled in northern France, where they became known as Normans. They also travelled to Iceland and Greenland, and, in 1003, reached Vinland (probably Newfoundland, Canada), almost 500 years before the Genoese explorer Columbus claimed to have discovered the same continent. A group of Vikings from Sweden, known as the Rus, set up trading posts at Novgorod and Kiev, giving their name – Russia – to the country they colonized.

Stories of the exploits of the Vikings were written by the people they attacked. These accounts naturally describe the Vikings as savage raiders, but they were also skilled craft-workers. The colonies they founded grew rich on trade, and the Vikings soon settled peacefully with the peoples they had once fought.

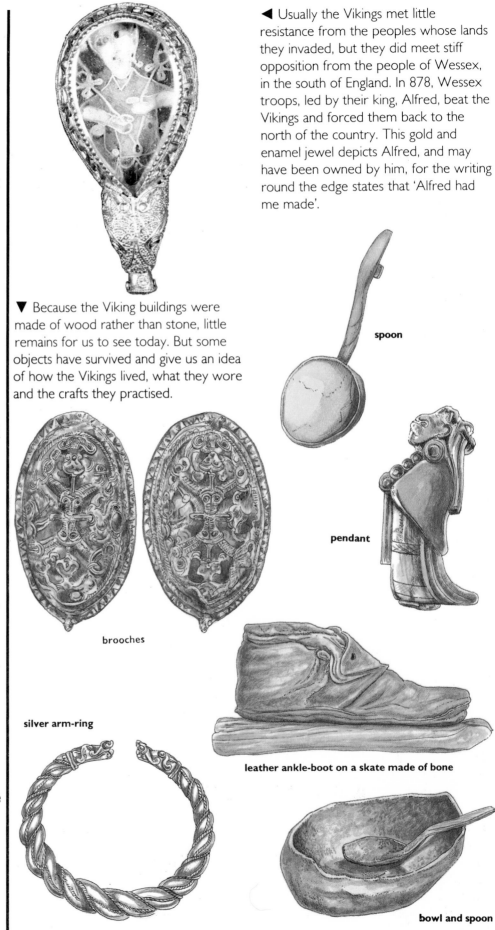

▼ Because the Viking buildings were made of wood rather than stone, little remains for us to see today. But some objects have survived and give us an idea of how the Vikings lived, what they wore and the crafts they practised.

◄ Usually the Vikings met little resistance from the peoples whose lands they invaded, but they did meet stiff opposition from the people of Wessex, in the south of England. In 878, Wessex troops, led by their king, Alfred, beat the Vikings and forced them back to the north of the country. This gold and enamel jewel depicts Alfred, and may have been owned by him, for the writing round the edge states that 'Alfred had me made'.

spoon

pendant

brooches

silver arm-ring

leather ankle-boot on a skate made of bone

bowl and spoon

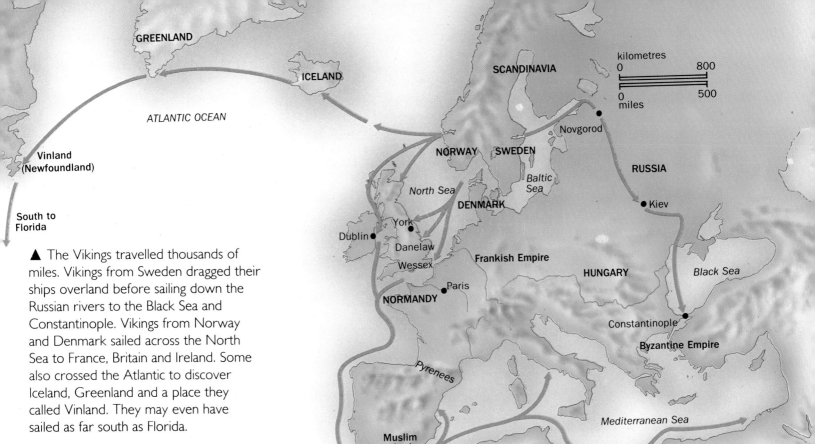

The Vikings travelled thousands of miles. Vikings from Sweden dragged their ships overland before sailing down the Russian rivers to the Black Sea and Constantinople. Vikings from Norway and Denmark sailed across the North Sea to France, Britain and Ireland. Some also crossed the Atlantic to discover Iceland, Greenland and a place they called Vinland. They may even have sailed as far south as Florida.

The Vikings could not read or write, so **sagas** or legends about their gods and heroes were learned by heart and handed down from parent to child by word of mouth. This wood carving shows the legendary hero Sigurd killing Fafnir the dragon.

The Vikings excelled at metalwork. This die, used to stamp an identifying picture on a metal sheet, shows two legendary warriors about to attack a ferocious beast.

The main reason for the success of the Vikings was the speed and seaworthiness of their longboats. The Vikings believed that the spirits of past leaders lived in the boats. For this reason, they buried their leaders with their ships when they died. This longboat was made for a queen and was found preserved in the mud at Oseberg in Norway

Norman invaders

In 1066 Edward the Confessor, the King of England, died. He had no children to succeed him and so three people claimed the English throne. They were Harold, Earl of Wessex (who was Edward's choice as his successor), the King of Norway and William, Duke of Normandy, who was Edward's cousin. Harold was crowned king but immediately the other two **claimants** prepared to attack Harold and seize the throne.

The King of Norway was the first to attack. He sailed over the North Sea with an army and landed in the north of England. There he was quickly defeated by Harold and killed in battle. But then William, Duke of Normandy, landed with a large army on the south coast of England. William was a descendant of the Viking invaders of northern France who had settled there in 911 and had become known as Normans. William claimed that Harold had once promised to support his claim to be king. Harold headed south to fight William's army but was defeated by them at a battle outside Hastings. William 'the Conqueror' then marched to London and was crowned King of England on Christmas Day, 1066.

William set about controlling his new kingdom by building fortified castles and giving lands and titles to his Norman followers. He soon overcame English opposition to his rule and ruled securely until the time of his death in 1087.

▲ The Bayeux Tapestry tells the story of the Norman invasion of England. The tapestry is more than 70 metres long and was made soon after the invasion in 1066. This section shows the Norman fleet crossing the English Channel.

◀ The kings of England were also dukes of Normandy and acquired further land in France through marriage. By 1154, they ruled over a greater area of France than the French king.

◀ In 1086 William the Conqueror ordered that a list be made of all the landowners in his new kingdom. The list took a year to compile and the results were recorded in the Domesday Book (in fact, two volumes). Domesday means 'Doomsday', or 'day of judgement'.

Castles

▲ Laying siege to a castle

The lord or **baron** of an area built a castle to defend the surrounding countryside, administer his lands and to provide a safe home for his family to live in. A castle was therefore a military barracks, an office and a house. The castle was protected from attack by a moat full of water which could only be crossed by a drawbridge. This would be raised in times of danger. A high wall surrounded an inner courtyard where there were stables for horses and living quarters for soldiers. Local people could bring their animals into the courtyard if they were attacked. At the centre of the castle stood the keep, a fortified house in which the lord and lady of the castle lived.

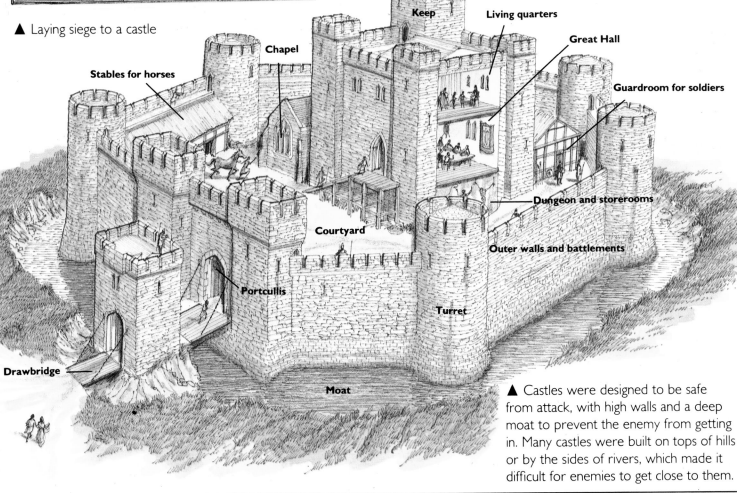

Keep

Living quarters

Great Hall

Chapel

Guardroom for soldiers

Stables for horses

Dungeon and storerooms

Courtyard

Outer walls and battlements

Portcullis

Turret

Drawbridge

Moat

▲ Castles were designed to be safe from attack, with high walls and a deep moat to prevent the enemy from getting in. Many castles were built on tops of hills or by the sides of rivers, which made it difficult for enemies to get close to them.

The Crusades

From about 200, Christian pilgrims from Europe travelled to Jerusalem and other parts of the Holy Land to worship in the places where Christianity had begun. But from 638, the Holy Land was controlled by Muslim Arabs. At first the Muslims did not interfere with the pilgrims, but in 1071 the Turks conquered the area. They attacked and killed the pilgrims and prevented Christians from worshipping in Jerusalem.

In 1095, Pope Urban the Second called on all Christians to go on **crusades** to the Holy Land to fight a holy war against the Turks. Within a year, a large army from all over Europe had gathered at Constantinople. When the Crusaders reached the Holy Land in 1099, they captured Jerusalem and set up several Christian kingdoms in the area.

Nine further Crusades were organized between 1147 and 1271 but none was as successful as the first. After Jerusalem was recaptured by the Muslims in 1187, a Children's Crusade attempted to recapture it in 1212. But the children were not armed and most were sold into slavery before they even reached the Holy Land. In 1291 the Christians were finally thrown out of the Holy Land.

The Crusades failed for many reasons. The Crusaders were often poorly equipped, and they frequently quarrelled among themselves. Many had gone to the Holy Land to make themselves rich, not to defend their religion.

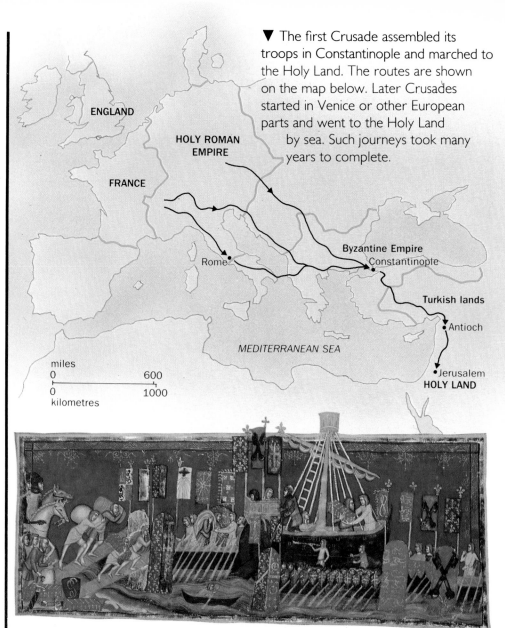

▼ The first Crusade assembled its troops in Constantinople and marched to the Holy Land. The routes are shown on the map below. Later Crusades started in Venice or other European parts and went to the Holy Land by sea. Such journeys took many years to complete.

ENGLAND

HOLY ROMAN EMPIRE

FRANCE

Rome

Byzantine Empire
Constantinople

Turkish lands

Antioch

MEDITERRANEAN SEA

miles
0 _____ 600
0 _____ 1000
kilometres

Jerusalem
HOLY LAND

▲ Embarking stores and provisions for a Crusade.

◀ Krak des Chevaliers (Castle of the Knights) in Syria was one of the strongest of the Crusader castles, built to guard the routes from the East to the Mediterranean coast.

◀ A knight would consider the rescue of a damsel in distress as a great honour. The highest duty of a knight was to protect vulnerable people.

▼ As part of the tournament splendid banquets were held for the knights, lords and ladies. After the meal the guests performed dances.

At the time of the Crusades, warfare was considered a worthwhile occupation and young men spent many hours practising the skills they would need on the battlefield. Mock battles, or **tournaments**, were held where sword fights and other contests of skill took place. Strict rules regulated these contests because they could be dangerous. The young knights were carefully dressed in armour to prevent them getting hurt (above) and they fought on behalf of a woman who made sure that the contest was fair. The most important contest was the joust (right), where two mounted horsemen charged each other and tried to unseat their opponent with a lance.

27

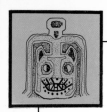

Empires beyond Europe

The Mayas of America

The peoples of the American continent remained isolated, apart from the Vikings' brief visit to north America in 1003. Many ideas and inventions that were developed in Europe and Asia, such as the wheel and the plough, remained unknown in America. Instead, the Americans developed their own **civilizations** without any outside contact.

Between 300 and 900, the Mayas of Central America built a flourishing empire, with huge cities dominated by massive temples where they worshipped their gods. They were skilled astronomers and mathematicians and were the only American people who could read or write. Another major civilization was the **city-state** of Teotihuacán, where 250,000 people lived. The city covered 13 square kilometres and was one of the largest in the world, even bigger than Rome, then the largest city in Europe. Both the Mayan Empire and the city of Teotihuacán started to decline in about 750. In 900 the Mayas were replaced as the greatest power in America by the Toltecs. In 1200 the Toltecs themselves were replaced by the Aztecs.

The other great civilizations in America were in the Andes Mountains to the south. There, up to 100,000 people lived in

continues on page 30

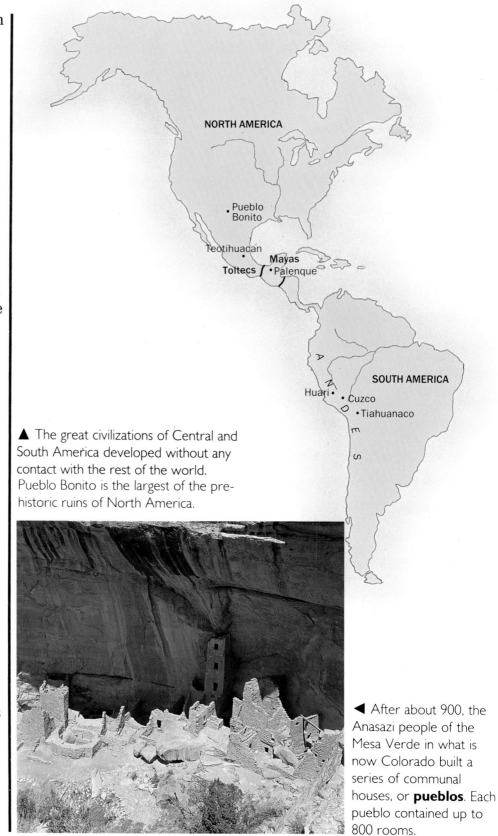

▲ The great civilizations of Central and South America developed without any contact with the rest of the world. Pueblo Bonito is the largest of the pre-historic ruins of North America.

◄ After about 900, the Anasazi people of the Mesa Verde in what is now Colorado built a series of communal houses, or **pueblos**. Each pueblo contained up to 800 rooms.

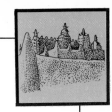

◀ At the centre of their cities the Mayas built pyramid-shaped temples surrounded by large palaces. This one is at Palenque in Mexico. Thousands of workers were required to construct these buildings. Many thousands more worked in the fields nearby to provide food for the workers.

▼ The Toltecs lived in central Mexico and governed a large empire which traded throughout the region. In their capital, Tula, they built many temples, guarded by stone statues of warriors.

The Mayan language
The Mayas wrote in a picture alphabet that no one else understood *(below)*. Only three of their documents survived the Spanish invasion in the 1530s. In the 1880s a scholar translated one document and began to decipher the Mayan language. However, many Mayan symbols are still not understood today.

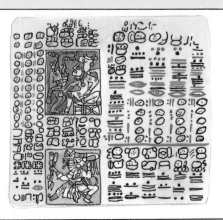

▲ The symbol of the cat appears throughout Central and South America on sculptures, carvings, pottery, and, as here, on a tapestry. In Peru, the city of Cuzco is thought to have been arranged in the shape of a puma.

continued from page 28

the cities of Tiahuanaco and Huari. Like the cities to the north, both Tiahuanaco and Huari were full of temples decorated with intricate carvings and both were the capitals of powerful empires.

Trade in Africa

South of the Sahara a number of countries developed and grew rich on trade and **commerce**. The kingdom of Ghana controlled the trade that flowed along the Niger River and sold spices and gold to the Arabs who crossed the Sahara. The Arabs brought their Muslim religion with them and gradually they converted the people of Ghana and the neighbouring areas to Islam. By 1300 the great trading cities of Jenne and Timbuctu were centres of Islamic learning and attracted scholars from all over west and north Africa.

On the east coast of Africa, the ports of Kilwa and Gedi exported ivory, spices and gold to Arabia, India and China, and imported carpets, ceramics and horses in return. In 1071, **ambassadors** were sent to China to establish trading contacts and fleets of Chinese **junks** visited the ports in 1418 and 1422, keen to buy the goods that were on sale.

Farther south, Great Zimbabwe was a wealthy state that grew rich on gold mining and cattle herding. The gold was taken overland to Sofala, where it was traded for beads, porcelain and other luxuries with the Arab traders who sailed south down the east coast of Africa.

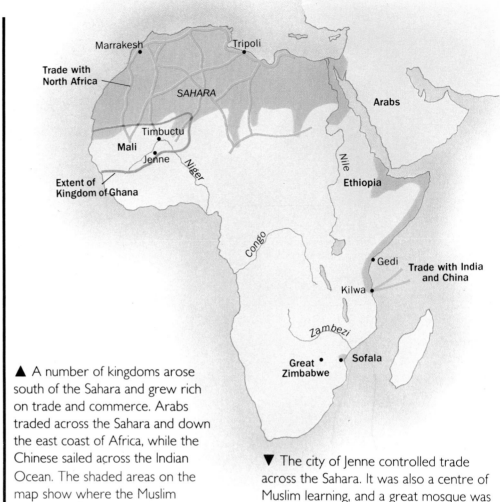

▲ A number of kingdoms arose south of the Sahara and grew rich on trade and commerce. Arabs traded across the Sahara and down the east coast of Africa, while the Chinese sailed across the Indian Ocean. The shaded areas on the map show where the Muslim religion was followed. The blue lines show trade routes.

▼ The city of Jenne controlled trade across the Sahara. It was also a centre of Muslim learning, and a great mosque was built there. Jenne is still a lively market town today.

▲ The cities of east Africa, such as Kilwa, conducted trade across the Indian Ocean with India and China. In 1414, east African ambassadors visited the Chinese Emperor with gifts, including a giraffe.

▼ Great Zimbabwe was the capital of a major trading empire that dominated southern Africa in the 1300s. The gold, iron and copper mined in the region were much in demand throughout Africa. Many of the ruins of the huge defensive walls and towers of the city can be seen today.

▲ The only practical way for Arab traders to cross the vast and inhospitable Sahara was by camel. Groups of traders travelled together for safety. These groups were called *caravans*. While some camels were ridden, many others were used to carry the traders' heavy loads. Although jeeps and lorries have now largely replaced them, camels are still used today for transport in the desert.

▲ Ethiopia was the only Christian country in Africa. In 1200, the kings of Ethiopia constructed 11 churches out of solid rock. The church of St George at Lalibela is shaped like a cross and, in common with the other churches, is still in use today.

Mongol invasions

The Mongols were tribes of nomads from the steppes or plains of central Asia. The different tribes often quarrelled among themselves, and it was not until 1206 that one of their leaders, Temujin, was proclaimed supreme ruler. He took the name Genghis Khan, which means 'Prince of all that lies between the Oceans', and his forces soon began to conquer the surrounding countries.

In 1211 the Mongols invaded China and captured its capital Beijing (Peking) in 1215. They then turned west and by 1223 had conquered central Asia. Genghis Khan died in 1227 but his son Ogedei continued the conquests in Russia, Hungary and on the shores of the Adriatic Sea. The Mongols had an army of 150,000 men and there was no power in Europe capable of stopping them. But then Ogedei died and the Mongols retreated.

Under their new leader Mongke, the Mongols captured Baghdad in 1258 and would have overrun the rest of the Islamic world had not Mongke also died. His successor was Kublai Khan, but he was less warlike and spent his life uniting the vast country of China. He allowed the Mongol Empire to break up into smaller sections.

At its height in 1279, the Mongol Empire stretched from the Baltic Sea to the Pacific Ocean, and from the Persian Gulf to the Arctic Circle. It was the biggest empire the world had ever seen.

▲ The Mongols were excellent riders and were able to cover up to 160 kilometres a day on their small and speedy horses. They fought with sharp arrows that could penetrate armour.

▼ In 1271, the Venetian traveller Marco Polo left Venice to visit China. He stayed in China for 20 years and met Kublai Khan, its ruler. Below is an illustration from the book he wrote about his travels. It shows gifts beings presented to 'the Great Khan'.

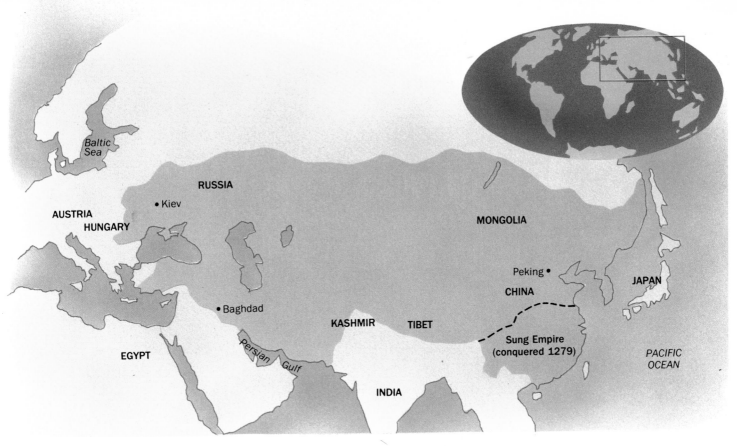

Baltic
Sea

RUSSIA

AUSTRIA
HUNGARY

• Kiev

MONGOLIA

Peking •

CHINA

JAPAN

• Baghdad

KASHMIR   TIBET

Sung Empire
(conquered 1279)

PACIFIC
OCEAN

EGYPT

Persian

Gulf

INDIA

▲ The Mongol Empire was the largest
empire the world had ever seen. At its
greatest extent it stretched across Asia
into eastern Europe and sent expeditions
of conquest into Austria, Egypt, India,
Java and Japan.

◄ The Mongols lived in yurts, or tents.
The yurts were made of skins or woven
cloth stretched over a wooden frame
and they were decorated with brightly
coloured rugs. They may not look strong
but they were warm enough to keep out
the cold of winter. Some tribes in
Afghanistan still live in yurts today.

33

The Growth of Trade

Wars in Europe

In 1200 Europe was divided quite differently from how it is today. Spain was divided into four different countries, one of which, Granada, was ruled by the Moors of north Africa. Some areas of France were ruled by the kings of England, while Germany, the Netherlands, Switzerland, Austria and northern Italy were all part of the Holy Roman Empire. Italy was divided into many small city-states, while in eastern Europe the constant wars meant that the borders of the countries were always changing.

The most powerful ruler in western Europe was the **Pope** As the head of the Roman Catholic Church, the Pope ruled over the wealthiest organization in western Europe. The Church had vast amounts of land, with estates in many different countries, and everybody was a member of the Roman Catholic Church. The Pope therefore had great influence over how the various European countries conducted their affairs.

This vast power brought the Pope into conflict with the Holy Roman Emperor, who claimed to be the leader of western Europe. The Pope had the right to crown the Emperor and used this right to assert his superiority over the Emperor and all other rulers. But the Emperor wanted to be

continues on page 36

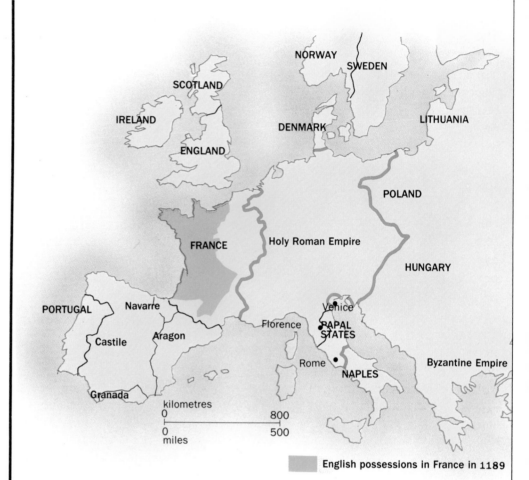

English possessions in France in 1189

▲ In 1200, Europe was a patchwork of different states that were often at war with each other. The Holy Roman Empire consisted of numerous small states held together by the Holy Roman Emperor and the Pope. Quarrels between these two powerful rulers dominated European history at this time.

▶ In order to govern their countries better, many European kings summoned parliaments. These meetings were composed of nobles and other high-ranking people from each town. They levied (collected) taxes on behalf of the king and helped him administer the country. The English parliament (right) was summoned by Edward the First in 1295 and consisted of two knights from each county and two representatives from each town.

1200–1450

The Black Death

The Black Death

The Black Death was a plague spread by fleas which lived on both rats and humans. No one knows where the plague started, but it was probably brought from Asia into Europe by rat-infested ships that traded across the Mediterranean. The plague arrived in Sicily in 1347 and then spread slowly northwards throughout the rest of Europe, reaching Scandinavia by 1353. Its effect was devastating. Almost everyone who caught the plague – perhaps one third of the total population of Europe – died. Whole towns and villages were wiped out and harvests were left to rot in the fields. Only a few areas were unaffected, because they managed to isolate themselves and prevent the rats from spreading the disease.

Durham 1349
London 1349
Paris 1348
Venice 1348
Marseilles 1347
Rome 1348
Seville 1348
Sicily 1347
Constantinople 1347
Southern Russia 1345
From Asia
Mediterranean Sea
0 kilometres 800
0 miles 500

▼ The Black Death killed almost everybody who caught it. It was often portrayed in pictures of the time as a dead person riding a horse, killing both rich and poor as it swept across the land.

▲ The Black Death probably came from Asia to Europe in 1347. It was carried by fleas that lived on rats, and on humans.

The Peasants' Revolt

Many other disasters struck Europe after 1300. A series of bad harvests led to widespread famine. Outbreaks of smallpox and influenza killed many people. Food prices rose because there were fewer people working on the land to produce the food. Across Europe, peasants demanded higher wages and violent demonstrations broke out in many countries. The most serious was in England, where wages were held down by law. In 1380, taxes were increased and many peasants revolted. Led by Wat Tyler, the peasants marched on London in 1381 and demanded changes in their working conditions. But Wat Tyler was killed and the revolt was put down with great severity.

continued from page 34

independent of the Pope. As a result, the two frequently quarrelled and at times fighting broke out between them.

Daily life

The quarrel between the Holy Roman Emperor and the Pope had little impact on the daily lives of most men and women. For them, the most important thing was to produce enough food to eat.

At this time, almost everybody lived and worked on the land under a system known as the **Feudal System**, from the Latin word *feudum* meaning 'control'. The feudal system began in France in about 750 and soon spread across Europe. Each king granted land to his most powerful **barons** or lords, who swore an oath of loyalty and agreed to fight for the king if he needed their support. The barons then divided this land into manors.

The one group of people who did not own any land were the **villeins** or peasants. The lords of the manor gave the peasants strips of land to farm for themselves, but in return they had to work in their master's fields, and give him some of their produce each year. The peasants grew crops such as wheat, barley and beans, and grazed pigs. The Feudal System survived in Russia and eastern Europe until the 1800s. In western Europe, however, it began to collapse in the 1300s when more and more people began to work in the towns where the Feudal System did not apply.

▲ The first modern European bank was established in Venice in 1171 in order to lend money to the government. Banks were soon formed in every major European city, for they helped develop trade and commerce. Merchants used the banks to deposit and invest their money safely.

◄ The most important building in people's lives was the church. Everyone went to church and the local priest was often the most important member of the community. In bigger towns and cities, cathedrals were built to show off the wealth and power of the church. These cathedrals took many years to build and employed numerous local craftworkers. Stonemasons, wood carvers and glassmakers all helped decorate the cathedral with sculptures and coloured glass.

► Harvesting was a laborious task, requiring every man, woman and child to help. The barley or rye that was harvested went to make bread for the peasants, who also lived on eggs, cheese, milk and the occasional chicken or pig. The nobles ate much better, and used wheat for their bread.

▼ In this gold and silver mine in central Europe, the miners are shown wearing white so that they can be seen in the dark. Above ground people crush and wash the minerals while others sell them (top) under the supervision of royal controllers.

▼ In the bigger houses, servants were employed to cook and clean. This lady of the manor is giving her orders to her kitchen staff.

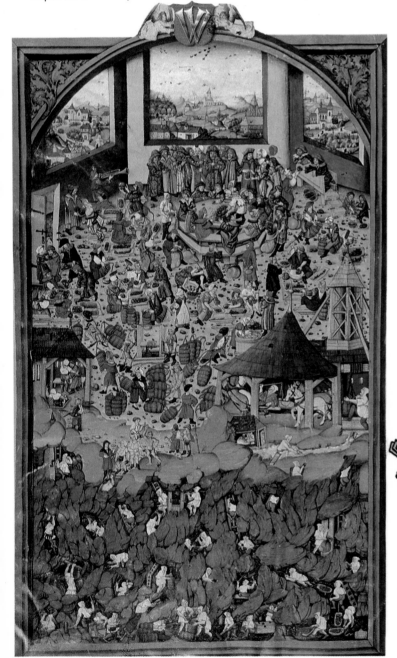

▼ Lepers and disabled people were common sights in many towns and villages, begging for food.

The Hanseatic League

In Europe, towns only started to grow in size after about 1200 when the threat of nomadic invasions had gone. New towns grew up along the trade routes where roads met or rivers could be crossed, while old towns expanded in the shadows of great cathedrals or fortified castles. These towns grew rich on trade. Many of them held fairs or markets where merchants could buy and sell their goods. Groups of craftworkers, such as goldsmiths or carpenters, formed associations known as **guilds** to protect their craft and train apprentices in their skills. These guilds grew rich and contributed much to the wealth of the towns.

In northern Europe, trade was dominated by the German towns around the south of the Baltic Sea. But this trade was often threatened by pirates at sea and robbers on land. In 1241, two of the towns, Hamburg and Lübeck, agreed to protect each other's merchants and safeguard their trade routes by setting up a *hanse*, or trading association. By 1300 all the German ports had set up hanses. Together they formed the Hanseatic League to safeguard their trading interests.

In 1400, at its greatest extent, the Hanseatic League had more than 150 members and traded throughout northern Europe. The Hanseatic traders brought copper, iron and herrings from Sweden and furs, grain and timber from eastern Europe and Russia. To the east, the

continues on page 40

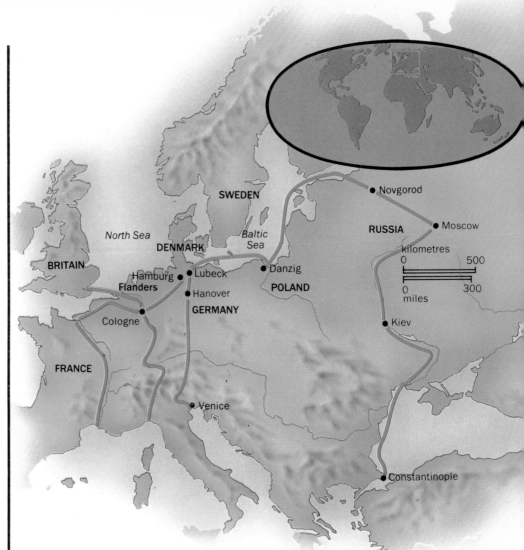

▲ Trade routes of the Hanseatic League. The Hanseatic League was the most important trading association in Europe. Its member towns stretched from Russia to Flanders and controlled trade in both the North and Baltic Seas.

▼ In the 1400s the fortified city of Novgorod in Russia was an important trading centre of the Hanseatic League. Amber, furs and wax were all traded here.

Inventions and Technology

Inventions came about over the course of many years as new ideas were used to improve old methods of working. Many of these inventions developed in China over hundreds of years and then slowly made their way to Europe, often through Arab influences. But printing and gunpowder remained unknown in Europe for many years after their first use in China, while the Chinese armies had no knowledge of the deadly longbow used by the English.

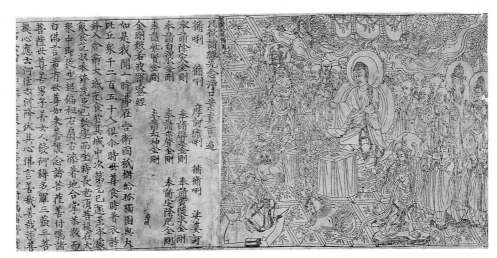

▲ The Diamond Sutra was printed in China in 868 and is the oldest surviving printed book in the world. The book is a collection of Buddhist prayers.

◀ The longbow was developed in England in the 1200s and was a lethal weapon because of the speed and accuracy of its delivery.

▼ The padded horse collar was originally a Chinese invention, introduced into Europe in the 900s. It enabled horses to be used on farms to pull heavy loads. Here a horse wearing a padded collar is pulling a harrow.

▼ The Chinese were skilled iron workers. Here a group of workers are forging a ship's anchor in the 1300s.

continued from page 38

merchants or traders of the League controlled the town of Novgorod in Russia, and dominated trade in that country. To the west, they traded across the North Sea with England. There the traders were known as *Easterlings*, because they came from the east. In time the word became shortened to 'sterling' and referred to the money the Hanse traders used. The word sterling is still in use today as the name for British currency.

Southern Europe

Venice was the most important trading city in southern Europe. As early as 900, the Venetians controlled most of the trade with the Middle East and China. They profited by equipping the fleets and armies that went on the Crusades, and by 1400 Venice had established an empire of trading ports throughout the eastern Mediterranean Sea. In this way it became the richest city in Europe.

China

In China too, towns were growing in size and importance. The population of China had reached over 110 million people by 1100, many more than lived in the whole of Europe. Cities such as Kaifeng became important trading and industrial centres, and by 1450 China had become the richest and most organized country in the world.

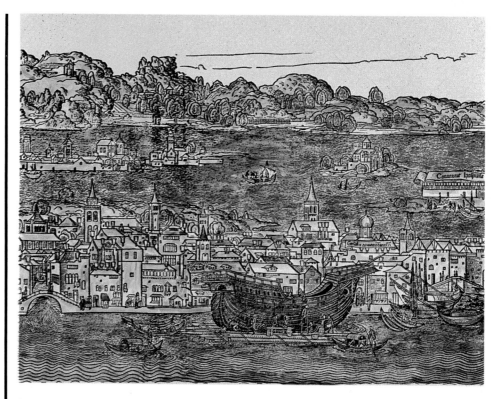

▲ For many years traders to the Middle East and China started their journeys from Venice. By 1400 it was a thriving port and the richest commercial city in Europe.

▼ Between 960 and 1127, the Chinese capital was at Kaifeng. It had a population of perhaps one million people and was a major centre of trade and industry. This scroll, drawn in about 1120, shows the bustle of the annual Spring Festival.

Glossary

Words in this book in **bold** are explained in the Glossary below.

Ambassador A person representing the interests of one country in another country.

Barbarians A term used by the Romans to describe the nomadic invaders of their empire.

Baron A powerful landowner whose lands were given by the king.

Caliph Religious ruler of a Muslim country.

Caste A group of people within the Hindu religion considered to have the same social status or class.

City-state A city that is also an independent country.

Civilization A developed and settled way of life including living in towns or cities.

Claimant A person who has a claim to the throne.

Colony A settlement abroad which is ruled or governed by the home country. Colonists are people who leave their home country to live in a colony.

Commerce Trade, or buying and selling.

Crusade Military expedition launched from Europe to recover the Holy Land from Muslim rule.

Culture Different kinds of learning such as art, literature, music and painting. Culture is also used to describe the way of life of the people of a country or region.

Dynasty A ruling family or series of rulers from one family.

Economy The financial and business affairs of a country.

Empire A group of countries under one ruler.

Feudal System A system of government based on land ownership and allegiance to the lord of the manor, the baron or the king.

Guild An association of workers sharing the same skill who join together to protect their interests and train new members.

Islam The religion of the Arabs and other peoples who worship Allah and follow Muhammad as his prophet. Followers of Islam are known as Muslims.

Junk Chinese sailing boat used to transport goods.

Kingdom A country ruled by a king or queen.

Minuscule Writing developed by scholars working for Charlemagne around 800.

Missionary A religious person who goes to another country to convert people to their religion.

Mosaic A picture made up of numerous pieces of different coloured stone or glass set in a wall, floor or ceiling.

Nomads People who move with their herds or flocks of animals in search of grazing land.

Pasture Land covered by grass used for grazing cattle or sheep.

Pilgrim A person who journeys to a religious site to worship there.

Pope Before the Reformation in the 1500s, head of the Christian Church in western Europe and based in Rome.

Pueblo Town or village built by native Americans.

Saga A long story concerning legendary or historical figures and events, passed down by word of mouth from parent to child.

Silk Road The main land route between China and Europe. Camel trains walked along it carrying travellers and goods for trade.

State A country or part of a country which governs its own affairs.

Steppes The grassy plains of central Asia.

Tax Money demanded by the ruler of a country to pay for the administration of government and sometimes for war.

Tournament A mock battle to test the strength and skills of knights and prepare them for warfare.

Trade The process of buying and selling goods.

Tribe A group of people often descended from the same person or sharing the same language and culture.

Villein A peasant tied to the land and under the authority of the lord of the manor.

Europe

The Middle East

Africa

Europe	The Middle East	Africa
452 Attila the Hun enters Italy.	**484** The Huns attack Persia and kill the Emperor.	**400** Axum in Ethiopia converts to Christianity.

452 Attila the Hun enters Italy.
455 Rome sacked by the Vandals.
476 The last Roman Emperor is overthrown.
527–65 Justinian attempts to recover the old Roman Empire for the Byzantine Empire.
711 Muslims invade Spain.
732 Muslim armies defeated in France at Poitiers.
*c.*750 The Feudal System starts to emerge.
771–814 Charlemagne rules vast Frankish Empire in western Europe.
793 Vikings start to raid Britain and France.
843, 870 Charlemagne's empire split into three parts.
962 Otto the First of Germany is crowned as the first Holy Roman Emperor.
1066 Normans invade and conquer England.
1154 Angevin Empire of England and France reaches its greatest extent.
1237 Mongols invade Russia, Hungary and Poland.
1241 Hamburg and Lübeck set up a trading association, leading to the formation of the Hanseatic League.
1337–1453 Hundred Years' War between England and France.
1347–53 Black Death sweeps Europe.

484 The Huns attack Persia and kill the Emperor.
527–65 Under Justinian, the Byzantine Empire conquers much of the Middle East.
579 At the end of the reign of Chosroes the First, the Sassanian Empire of Persia reaches its greatest extent.
622 Muhammad flees from Mecca to Medina.
630 Muhammad returns to Mecca and makes it the capital of his new empire.
632 Death of Muhammad and the start of Arab expansion throughout the Middle East.
642 The Arabs conquer Persia and overthrow the Sassanian Empire.
756 The Islamic Empire starts to break up into independent countries.
762 Baghdad is founded by Al-Mansur.
1096–9 The First Crusade captures Jerusalem and establishes a number of Christian states in the area.
1187 Jerusalem is recaptured from the Crusaders.
1258 The Mongols capture Baghdad.
1261 The Mongol advance in the Middle East is stopped by the Egyptians.
1291 The Crusaders are finally thrown out of the Holy Land.

400 Axum in Ethiopia converts to Christianity.
429 The Vandals overrun the Roman Empire in north Africa and set up their own kingdom.
535 The Byzantine Emperor Justinian conquers north Africa.
639 Arabs invade Egypt.
*c.*700 Whole of north Africa is now controlled by Arabs and converts to Islam.
*c.*700 Arab traders start to cross the Sahara and trade with the peoples to the south.
700–1200 Kingdom of Ghana, the first great African empire, grows rich on trade.
971 World's first university is founded in Cairo.
1071 East African ports of Kilwa and Gedi send ambassadors to China.
1190 Lalibela becomes king of Ethiopia and starts to build new churches.
1235 The Kingdom of Mali is established.
*c.*1250 The city of Jenne is founded.
*c.*1300 Great Zimbabwe emerges as a major trading empire.
1324 Mansa Musa, king of Mali, goes on a pilgrimage to Mecca and astounds everyone with his wealth.
1418, 1422 Chinese fleets visit east Africa in search of trade.

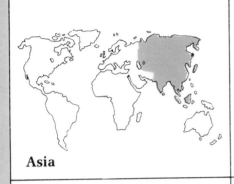		
Asia	**The Americas**	**Australasia**

Asia	The Americas	Australasia
535 Final collapse of Gupta Empire in India. **581** Sui Dynasty founded in China. **594** Buddhism becomes official religion of Japan. **618–907** T'ang Dynasty in China. **624** Buddhism becomes official religion of China. **802** The Angkor kingdom is established in Cambodia under the Khmer Dynasty. **868** The Diamond Sutra is printed in China. It is the world's oldest printed book. **960–1127** Sung Dynasty rules China from Kaifeng. **1206** Temujin becomes supreme ruler of the Mongols and takes the name Genghis Khan. **1211** Mongols invade China. **1264** Kublai Khan becomes ruler of China and sets up Yuan Dynasty in 1280 that lasts to 1368. **1271–95** The Venetian merchant Marco Polo travels across Asia to China. **1333** China suffers terrible drought, famine and floods, followed by the plague. Up to five million people die. **1368** Ming Dynasty takes over in China. **1369–1405** Tamerlane rules a new Mongol Empire based on Samarkand in central Asia. **1421** Beijing (Peking) becomes the capital of China.	***c*.300** The Mayan Empire begins. ***c*.600** Teotihuacán is at the height of its power. ***c*.600** Cities of Tiahuanaco and Huari in South America start to grow in size and importance. ***c*.750** Mayan Empire and Teotihuacán start to decline. ***c*.900** Anasazi peoples of north America build pueblos in the cliffs. ***c*.900** The Toltecs conquer the Mayas and build an empire in Central America. **1003** Vikings sail to Vinland (Newfoundland) and possibly explore coast as far south as Florida. ***c*.1200** Aztecs begin to establish an empire in Mexico. **1200** City of Cuzco is founded by the first Incas.	***c*.800** The Maoris arrive in New Zealand from the Pacific Islands.

Index

Page numbers in *italics* refer to
illustrations

A
Aachen (Germany) 20
Afghanistan 33
Africa 8, *9*, 11, 12, 16; trade 30–1
agriculture 36, 37, *37*, 39, *39*
Alexandria 9
Al-Mansur 17
Alfred, King 22, *22*
America 8, 28–9
Angles 11
Arabs 13, 16, 17, 22, 26; in Africa
    30, 31, *31*
architecture: Buddhist *18*; castles
    25, *26*; church *31*, *36*; Mayan *29*;
    monastic *15*; Roman *9*
arts and crafts: calligraphy *15*, *17*;
    carving/sculpture *8*, *10*, *14*, *19*,
    23, *29*; mosaics *11*, *13*; Sassanian
    9; Saxon *10*; Toltec *29*; Viking
    22, *23*
Asoka (ruler of India) 18
astronomers, Arab 17
Australia 8
Avars 20
Axum, kingdom of 9, *9*
Aztec Empire 8, 28

B
Baghdad 17, 32
banks 36, *36*
Barbarians 10–11
barons 25, 36
Bayeux Tapestry 24, *24*
Beijing (Peking) 32
Black Death 35, *35*
Book of Kells (manuscript) 15, *15*
books *15*, *16*, *20*, *24*, *32*, *39*
Borobudur (Java), temple at 18
Buddhism 14, 18–19, *18*
Bulgars 12
Burma 18
Byzantine Empire 12–13, 16

C
Cairo 17

calligraphy 15, *15*, 17, *17*
caravans (desert) 31, *31*
Carolingian Dynasty 20
Carthage 11
caste system, Hindu 18
castles 24, 25, *25*, *26*
cathedrals 36, *36*
Charlemagne 20
Children's Crusade 26
China 8, 9, 10, 21, 30, 31;
    Buddhism 18–19; cities 40;
    inventions 39, *39*; Mongols 32
Christianity 10, 12, 14–15, 31, *31*,
    34, *36*; Crusades 26–7
churches 13, *13*, 14, *14*, 31, *31*, 36,
    36
Clovis (Frankish king) 20
Columbus, Christopher 22
Constantine (Emperor of Rome) 12,
    14
Constantinople 12, *12*
Crusades 26–7, *26*, 40
Cuzco (Peru) 29

D
decimal system 13
Denmark 22, 23
dhows (ships) 21, *21*
Diamond Sutra 39, *39*
Diocletian (Emperor of Rome) 12
Domesday Book 24, *24*

E
Edward (the Confessor), King 24
Edward First, King 34, *34*
engineers, Arab 17
Ephesus (Turkey) 9
Ethiopia 31
Europe 8, 11, 20, 23, 34, 35, 36;
    Hanseatic League 38

F
fairs 21, *21*
famines 35
farming *see* agriculture
feudal system 36
footbinding (China) 19, *19*
France 16, 21, 22, 23, 24, 36
Franks 11, 16, 20

G
Gautama Siddhartha (Buddha) 18,
    19
Gedi (E. Africa) 30

Genghis Khan (Temujin) 32
Germany 38
Ghana, kingdom of 30
Granada (Spain) 34
Great Wall (China) 10
Great Zimbabwe 30, 31, *31*
Greek Fire 13, *13*
Greenland 22
Guatemala 8
guilds 38
gunpowder 39
Gupta Empire (India) 8, 10, 13

H
Hadrian's Wall 10
Hamburg 38
Han Dynasty (China) 8
Hanseatic League 38
Harold, Earl of Wessex 24
Hastings, Battle of 24
Hinduism 14, 18
Hitler, Adolf 20
Holy Land 26
Holy Roman Empire 20, 34, 36
Huari (S. America) 30
Hungary 32
Huns 10, 11

I
Iceland 22
India 8, 10, 13, 18
Indochina 18
Iona (Scotland) 14, *14*, 15
Ireland 22
Islam 14, 16, 26, 30, 32
Italy 12, 34

J
Japan 18
Java 18, *18*
Jenne (Kingdom of Mali) 30, *30*
Jerusalem 26
Jesus Christ 14
jousts 27, *27*
Judaism 14
Justinian, Emperor 12, 13, *13*
Jutes 11

K
Kaaba (Mecca) 16, *16*
Kaifeng (China) 40, *40*
Kiev 22, 23
Kilwa (E. Africa) 30, 31
knights 27, *27*

Acknowledgements

The publishers wish to thank the following for supplying photographs for this book:

Page 9 Sonia Halliday Photographs; 10 SCALA; 11 Michael Holford; 12 Bibliotheque Nationale, Ms Lat 4825 f37v; 13 Sonia Halliday Photographs; 14 SCALA; 15 Trinity College, Cambridge (left) Trinity College, Dublin (right); 16 ZEFA (top) British Museum (middle); 17 Bodleian Library, Ms Marsh 144 f.61 (top) Bodleian Library, Ms Lococke 37s f.3v4r (left) Werner Forman Archive (right); 18 The Hutchison Library; 19 Robert Harding Picture Library (top) ZEFA (left) The Mansell Collection (right); 21 Sonia Halliday Photographs; 22 Ashmolean Museum; 23 Werner Forman Archive (left) Universitets Oldsaksamling (right); 24 Michael Holford (top) Public Record Office (bottom); 25 By Courtesy of the Trustees of Sir John Soane's Museum; 26 Sonia Halliday Photographs; 27 Bodleian Library, Ms. Douce 195 fol.7; 28 ZEFA; 29 South American Pictures (top) Michael Holford (bottom); 30 ZEFA; 31 The Hutchison Library (top) Barbara Heller (bottom); 32 British Museum (top) Bodleian Library, Ms Bodley 264 fol.237 (bottom); 33 The Hutchison Library; 34 The Mansell Collection; 35 SCALA; 36 British Library, Ms Add 27695 fol.8 (top) National Bibliothek, Vienna; 37 The Mansell Collection (top) National Bibliothek, Vienna (bottom); 38 The Mansell Collection; 39 The British Library (top) Giraudon (bottom); 40 Ancient Art & Architecture Collection (top) Werner Forman Archive (bottom).

Overleaf: British Museum

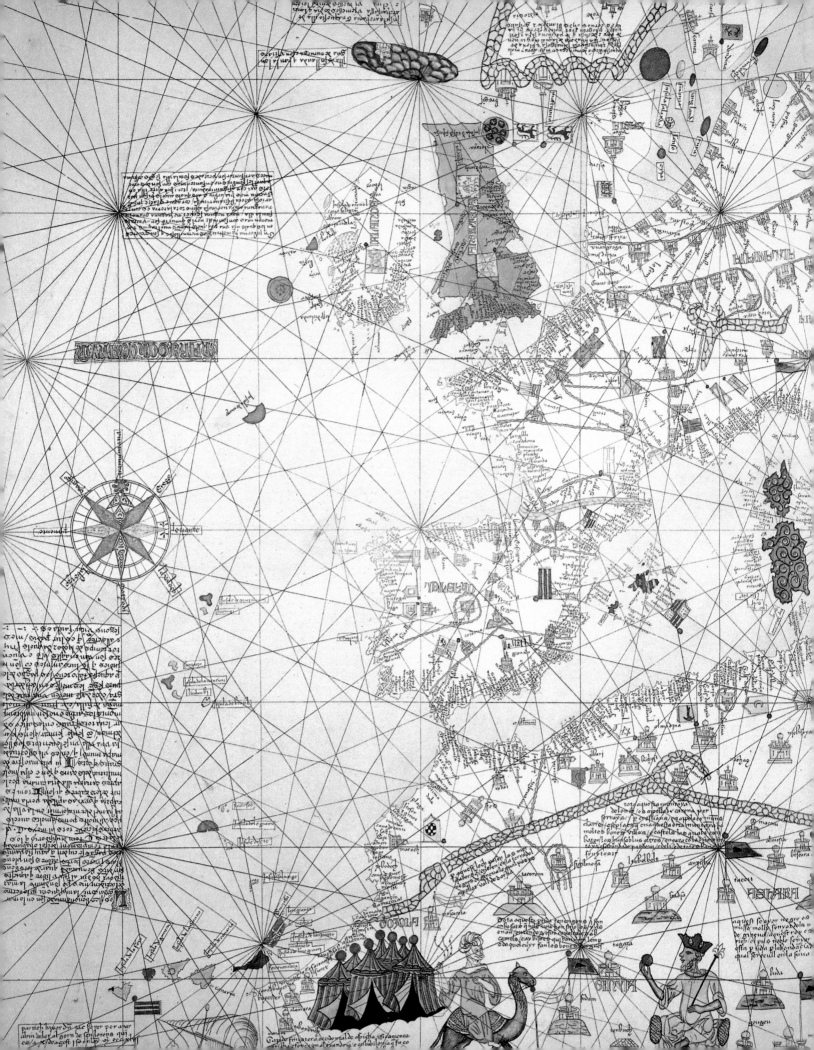

Previous Page: The Catalan map, made in 1375 by Abraham Cresques for the king of France. It is more accurate than many other maps of the time, since much of it was based on seamen's charts that had been drawn using compass bearings. The writings of Marco Polo were the main source of the information on Central Asia and China.